The Rapture:
Wise Up and Rise Up!

Rosamund Weissman

The Rapture:
Wise Up and Rise Up!

Published by Fresh Olive Press
www.fresholivepress.com

ISBN 978-1-8382347-3-7
First printing 2024
Printed in the United Kingdom

Cover image by Denise Cusack sourced from pexels.com

Contents

A word to the reader

This deeply practical publication is pertinent to both Christians and also to those from all faith backgrounds who are not yet born again. At the end of 2019, Covid suddenly appeared and within months made an unwelcome stamp on our lives and upon our society. There is something universally devastating coming soon. It will make lockdowns pale into insignificance. It will dramatically affect both believers and non-believers alike, and life as we know it now will never be the same again. This writing will still be relevant to many when that event takes place. Wise preparation is essential for each one of us. There is a prayer at the end if you are convicted of your own sin and desire to know God and to embark on a personal relationship with His divine Son, God in the flesh, the Lord Jesus Christ (*Yeshua Ha Mashiakh* in Hebrew) and be part of His family. It is also suitable if you hitherto have only given mental assent to the message of Jesus, yet now wish to cry out to God with a repentant heart to be saved from the just judgement of your sin through the shed blood of Jesus on the Cross.

Preface

We are living in dark days approaching the glorious return of the Light of the world. Truth is falling in our streets, evil is called good and good called evil. The earth is full of violence and ripe for God's judgement. We have the glorious hope of our future redemption. We are equipped with the Word of God, a lamp for our feet and a light for our path. We need not stumble amidst the darkness and confusion of this age, for "the path of the just is like the shining sun, that shines ever brighter unto the perfect day." Very soon, the people who live in darkness will see a great light. May we, the bride, be enlightened and fully prepared for our soon-coming Bridegroom, ever growing in sanctification and devotion. For "we know that when He is revealed, we shall be like Him, for we shall see Him as He is. And everyone who has this hope in Him purifies himself, just as He is pure."[1]

Introduction

The prophet Ezekiel was called by the Lord to be a watchman and to pass on to Israel the warnings he heard from the Lord. If he failed to warn the wicked that they would die, Ezekiel would have personal responsibility for their death. If one of his listeners disregarded the warning, their blood would be upon their own head. It must have been a heavy and extremely unpopular burden for Ezekiel to bear. Since we are at the end of the age, there is undoubtedly a watchman's warning to be given.

Christians are deeply divided in their opinion about the timing of the Rapture, the snatching away of believers, as described in 1 Thessalonians 4:16-18: "the dead in Christ will rise first. Then we who are alive and remain shall be caught up

---

[1] John 8:12, Isaiah 59:14, Isaiah 5:20, Genesis 6:13, Ephesians 4:4, Psalm 119:105, Proverbs 4:18, Isaiah 9:2, 1 John 3:2-3

together with them in the clouds to meet the Lord in the air. And thus we shall always be with the Lord. Therefore comfort one another with these words." Will this comforting reunion with the resurrected dead to meet Jesus in the sky happen before the last seven years of this age (pre-tribulation), at the end of that time (post-tribulation), or at some point during this time of trouble coming upon the earth in the Last Days (mid-tribulation)?

I have heard it said that irrespective of which view one takes on the timing of the Rapture, there are biblical problems. Indeed, over my nearly 50 years of being a Messianic Jewish believer in the Lord Jesus, with a long-term interest in the End Times, I have shifted positions several times on the matter. Over the course of the decades, I have moved from post-tribulation to pre-tribulation, then to pre-wrath, and more recently to partial pre-tribulation. I have, in my time, been an avid reader of the popular "Left Behind" series by the late Tim LaHaye (staunchly pre-tribulation). Subsequently, I have learned much from the writings and teaching of Joel Richardson (post-tribulation) and, over the last couple of years or so, my favourite online end-times teacher has been Nelson Walters (pre-wrath). In recent days, I have felt the Lord impress upon me a different view, which forms the subject of this writing. I am not attempting a rigorous theological treatment of all the Rapture theories. Whichever view you favour, I trust you will find this to be a timely challenge to make spiritual preparation for what lies ahead. Search the Scriptures to see whether the ideas I present are supported by the Word of God. "It is the glory of God to conceal a matter, but the glory of kings is to search out a matter."[2]

Many Bible teachers and ministers have been embarrassed in recent years to give instruction on the doctrine of the Rapture. Much of this stems from an understandable desire to distance themselves from the legacy of individuals such as the late Harold Camping. As part of a 100 million US dollar campaign, Camping broadcast on his Family Radio network, initially predicting the Rapture would occur in September 1994, and then subsequently proclaiming the correct date would be in May, then October, 2011.[3] After the May 2011 date failed to materialise, the Daily Mail[4] featured a photograph of a man standing outside an atheist "Rapture party" holding a billboard proclaiming the mocking message, "The End was Nigh or so they say..." But, in our desire to distance ourselves from such ridicule, are we throwing the baby out with the proverbial bathwater? Is the Lord pleased with such an attitude? Is this a wise or foolish response to public false date-setting predictions? Surely, we want to be among those who are eligible for the crown of righteousness because we have craved His appearing.[5]

[2] Proverbs 25:2
[3] www.christianitytoday.com "Died: Harold Camping, Christian Radio Host Who Predicted the World's End"
[4] www.dailymail.co.uk/news/article "Paradise postponed: World will now end on OCTOBER 21 says preacher who was surprised we all survived Saturday"
[5] 2 Timothy 4:8

Rapture in the Old Testament

We will start our consideration of this matter by looking at Old Testament allusions to the Rapture. Augustine, the bishop of Hippo from 396 to 430, said: "The new is in the old concealed; the old is in the new revealed." We read: "Enoch walked with God; and he was not, for God took him."[6] He is also referred to in Hebrews 11:5, where it is explained that Enoch was taken owing to his testimony that he pleased God. Enoch was snatched away (or raptured) because of the quality of his walk with the Lord. The other Old Testament character who was taken up without dying was the giant of faith, Elijah, who went up by a whirlwind into heaven.[7]

Then, we move on to Daniel, who describes a great divide among the dead. "And many of those who sleep in the dust of the earth shall awake, some to everlasting life, some to shame and everlasting contempt."[8] The first part of the verse refers to the Rapture, when the dead in Christ rise. Then there will be a long gap before the fulfilment of the second part of the verse. This will take place after the millennial reign of Jesus, when the remainder of the dead will be awakened in preparation for the Great White Throne Judgement.

Next, we come to more subtle references to the Rapture in the Old Testament. The Song of Solomon presents the king bridegroom escorted by 60 warriors, and perfumed with myrrh

---

[6] Genesis 5:24
[7] 2 Kings 2:11
[8] Daniel 12:2

and frankincense.[9] His delight in his beautiful bride is described in great detail, even after she had expressed reservations about being too dark:[10] "You are all fair, my love, and there is no spot in you."[11] Notice how the bride is spotless and how besotted the king is with her. "Come with me from Lebanon, my spouse, with me from Lebanon... you have ravished my heart, my sister, my spouse; you have ravished my heart with one look of your eyes, with one link of your necklace. How fair is your love, my sister, my spouse!"[12] The bridegroom describes her as "the fairest among women."[13] King Solomon represents the Lord Jesus, our heavenly Bridegroom. This king is single-minded in being united in intimacy with his beloved bride (a type of the church). He yearns for them to be together, and he urges her to come away with him, prefiguring the Rapture. "Rise up, my love, my fair one, and come away. For lo, the winter is past, the rain is over and gone. The flowers appear on the earth; the time of singing has come, and the voice of the turtledove is heard in our land...O my dove, in the clefts of the rock, in the secret places of the cliff, let me see your face, let me hear your voice; for your voice is sweet, and your face is lovely."[14]

There are two contrasting responses in Song of Solomon from the bride, which may have something to teach us about our attitude to the Rapture. At the start of the book, she is longing to be taken away by the bridegroom: "Draw [or take]

---

[9] Song of Solomon 3:7
[10] Song of Solomon 1:6
[11] Song of Solomon 4:7
[12] Song of Solomon 4:7-10
[13] Song of Solomon 1:8
[14] Song of Solomon 2: 10-14

me away!"[15] The bride-to-be has been working in the vineyard. We too work in the vineyard of the Lord and we also must share the concern for fruitfulness, for removal of the little foxes which spoil the vines.[16] We have to deal with sin and oppression as soon as we are aware of it, not forgetting that neglected little foxes in our lives grow into big foxes, the classic example being the root of bitterness by which many will be defiled.[17] There is a positive and eager response from her, described in passages like, "Let him kiss me with the kisses of his mouth—for your love is better than wine. Because of the fragrance of your good ointments, your name is ointment poured forth; therefore the virgins love you. Draw me away!"[18] Her mind was controlled by the Spirit, which is life and peace.[19] On the other hand, we see the opposite and indifferent reaction to the bridegroom's wooing: "I have taken off my robe; how can I put it on again? I have washed my feet; how can I defile them?"[20] The bride took her time in chapter 5 before she decided to open the door, and sadly by the time she opened for her beloved, he had turned away and was gone. She searched for him but could not find him.[21] The bride took too long to respond to the call of her bridegroom. She subsequently regretted being left behind on her own. She allowed herself to be distracted by earthly concerns, for her mind to be set on the flesh, which is hostility (or enmity) towards God.[22] Those

---

[15] Song of Solomon 1:4
[16] Song of Solomon 1:6, 2:15
[17] Hebrews 12:15
[18] Song of Solomon 1:2-4
[19] Romans 8:6
[20] Song of Solomon 5:3
[21] Song of Solomon 5:6
[22] Romans 8:7

in authority, whom she may have expected to protect her, treated her badly: "The watchmen who went about the city found me. They struck me, they wounded me."[23] This may well reflect how authorities will treat Christians during the Tribulation period.

Understandably, this picture of us being the bride of Christ is a challenge for many men. Conversely, some women may struggle with apparently bloodthirsty verses about Jesus defeating His foes as part of His return at the end of the age. One such example is the Lord's coming from Edom, His garments red and stained with the blood of His enemies.[24] He is not merely the Bridegroom awaiting His Bride. He has another side to His end-times role. He is also *Ish Milkhamah* (Hebrew for Man of war).[25] Another of His names is *Jehovah Tsva'ot*, meaning Lord of the armies of heaven. The juxtaposition of our Saviour being both the coming Bridegroom and the One who punishes His enemies is best summed up in the title of a beautiful song available on YouTube, "Romanced by a Warrior."[26] Whether we are male or female, we need to think in terms of a romantic everlasting relationship with the divine Son of God. He endured the cross and despised its shame for the joy set before Him.[27] We are a part of that joy. He is also soon returning to take revenge on His enemies. This is who we need to focus upon, rather than exhaust our personal supply of the oil of the Holy Spirit upon a never-ending list of

---

[23] Song of Solomon 5:7
[24] Isaiah 63:1-3
[25] Exodus 15:3
[26] First Love - Romanced by a Warrior (extended + spontaneous worship) Jesus Communion
[27] Hebrews 12:2

religious Christian duties. "O foolish Galatians! Who has be-witched you...did you receive the Spirit by the works of the law, or by the hearing of faith? Are you so foolish? Having begun in the Spirit, are you now being made perfect by the flesh?"[28]

Wise and Foolish Virgins

The New Testament is far clearer in its dealing with the subject of the readiness of the bride. We need to take some time to focus on the clearest relevant presentation – the parable of the five wise and five foolish virgins who took lamps in order to go out and meet the bridegroom. "Those who were foolish took their lamps and took no oil with them, but the wise took oil in their vessels with their lamps. But while the bridegroom was delayed, they all slumbered and slept. And at midnight a cry was heard: 'Behold, the bridegroom is coming; go out to meet him!' Then all those virgins arose and trimmed their lamps. And the foolish said to the wise, 'Give us some of your oil, for our lamps are going out.' But the wise answered, saying, 'No, lest there should not be enough for us and you; but go rather to those who sell, and buy for yourselves.' And while they went to buy, the bridegroom came, and those who were ready went in with him to the wedding; and the door was shut. Afterward the other virgins came also, saying, 'Lord, Lord,

---

[28] Galatians 3:1-3

open to us!' But he answered and said, 'Assuredly, I say to you, I do not know you.'"[29]

It is significant that there were 10 virgins. According to Alfred Edersheim[30] (1825-1889), the Hebrew Christian commentator, 10 was the number required to be present at a marriage ceremony in New Testament times. It was the custom to carry 10 or so lamps in the bridal procession. Even to the modern Jewish mind, 10 also suggests a congregation, due to the requirement for a quorum (*minyan*) of 10 adult male Jews to conduct various religious activities including reciting certain prayers and the priestly blessing.[31] The lamps held by the virgins were not small personal clay oil lamps often depicted by artists in paintings of the scene. Instead they were public lanterns, held up for all to see in the bridal procession.[32]

The size of the lamp, together with the long wooden pole, is most relevant to our study. Some effort was involved in carrying such a contraption. This is a reminder of where Jesus instructs us: "If anyone desires to come after Me, let him deny himself, and take up his cross, and follow Me."[33] Furthermore, the public nature of the torch being held brings to mind, "that you may become blameless and harmless, children of God without fault in the midst of a crooked and perverse generation, among whom you shine as lights in the world."[34] Wise

[29] Matthew 25:6-12
[30] "The Life and Times of Jesus the Messiah" Hendrickson Publications
[31] Chabad.org "Minyan: The Prayer Quorum"
[32] Distinction explained by Nelson Walters in YouTube video; "Unlocking the Mystery of the Ten Virgins Parable: They Carry TORCHES not Lamps and What it MEANS Nelson Walters 2023"
[33] Matthew 16:24
[34] Philippians 2:15

virgins in these Last Days are visibly different to the world around them and do not compromise to fit in. They are bold and take personal responsibility to prepare for what is ahead, rather than passively assuming that their Christian leader, fellowship or religious duties will suffice to provide spare oil.

In modern Western culture, if guests are held up on their way to the wedding ceremony or the celebratory meal that typically follows, they can usually quietly sneak in late to join the event. However, ancient Jewish wedding customs dictated that no one else could enter the wedding celebrations once the door was shut.[35] Not one of us can afford to be casual about being ready to be admitted to the marriage supper of the Lamb. This is not the time or place to be "fashionably late." We want to be safely behind those doors during the time of Tribulation and the outpouring of the wrath of God: "Come, my people, enter your chambers, and shut your doors behind you; hide yourself, as it were, for a little moment, until the indignation [or wrath] is past. For behold, the Lord comes out of His place to punish the inhabitants of the earth for their iniquity."[36]

Each of the 10 were virgins and this implies that they were Christians set apart for the Lord: "For I am jealous for you with godly jealousy. For I have betrothed you to one husband, that I may present you as a chaste virgin to Christ."[37] Furthermore, each virgin had oil to start with because the lamps were initially alight. Oil is widely understood to represent the Holy

---

[35] "Ready or Not – He is Coming" Stephanie Cottam
www.bereanbiblechurch.org "The Wise and Foolish Virgins"
[36] Isaiah 26:20-21
[37] 2 Corinthians 11:2

Spirit and the lamp the word of God.[38] However, as the coming of the bridegroom grew close, the foolish virgins ran out of oil, meaning that they still read their Bibles (the lamp), yet their portion of the Holy Spirit (the oil) to illuminate the Scriptures ran low and was finally extinguished. Each of the virgins was waiting for the return of the bridegroom. Most relevant for our study is the fact that although the foolish went out to purchase some oil, there was neither opportunity nor time to complete this transaction before the door to the wedding feast was permanently shut. Now if the foolish virgins were simply unsaved people reading their Bibles, as many believe, then it would not take long for them to repent and pray to receive the Lord in salvation.

How can we get oil in our lamps today?

What aspect of having the Holy Spirit in our lives takes time and the investment of resources? What does the costly oil represent? There are those who believe that it points to the oil of intimacy which comes from spending time with the Lord.[39] This is deeply challenging because growing in intimacy takes time, and the time has to be taken from something else. We are accustomed to the Western church, with which most of us will identify, having available a lavish supply of food, entertainment and material blessings; rich in these things but poor

---

[38] For a full discussion see https://www.bibletools.org for the oil. Psalm 119:105 re the lamp.
[39] Mike Connell Ministries "Oil of Intimacy" YouTube, Restoration House Calgary website

in time. "Because you say, 'I am rich, have become wealthy, and have need of nothing'—and do not know that you are wretched, miserable, poor, blind, and naked—I counsel you to buy from Me gold refined in the fire, that you may be rich; and white garments, that you may be clothed, that the shame of your nakedness may not be revealed; and anoint your eyes with eye salve, that you may see."[40] Notice how the lukewarm church is also told to go and buy (or invest resources in) something valuable: gold. We are exhorted to redeem the time because the days are evil.[41] It will help if we keep in mind the warning not to love the world nor the things in the world: "For all that is in the world—the lust of the flesh, the lust of the eyes, and the pride of life—is not of the Father but is of the world and the world is passing away, and the lust of it; but he who does the will of God abides forever."[42]

We must remember that we are the bride of the Saviour, who is returning soon for us. His deep desire is to present us to Himself a glorious church, without spot (sometimes translated "stain") or wrinkle, such that we should be holy and without blemish (or defect or fault).[43] We take care of our clothes to protect them from stains, we wash them, and we iron wrinkled garments. How much more will a bride in love with her bridegroom make sure that she is ready, make-up and nail varnish skilfully applied, hair looking beautiful and attired in attractive and spotless garments for her wedding day? Picture an engaged couple where the woman spends all of her spare time decorating their future home together, and is always too busy

---

[40] Revelation 3:17-18
[41] Ephesians 5:16
[42] 1 John 2:15-17
[43] Ephesians 5:27

and distracted working in this way to spend time developing her relationship with her fiancé. Subsequently, he discovers that his bride-to-be is planning to save time by turning up for their wedding without bothering to wash and style her hair, wearing a crumpled, stained dress that she has been keeping in the bottom of a cupboard. Would we blame the bridegroom for concluding that she is not serious about her commitment to their union and deciding to call off the wedding? She may object, saying, "look how hard I worked so that you would be happy." He on the other hand may be feeling neglected, hurt and rejected, and explain that he wants a marriage based on a close relationship rather than fulfilling duties for one another.

We are told how we should be dressed for the wedding supper of the Lamb: "Let us be glad and rejoice and give Him glory, for the marriage of the Lamb has come, and His wife has made herself ready. And to her it was granted to be arrayed in fine linen, clean and bright, for the fine linen is the righteous acts of the saints."[44] This accords with Romans 13:14: "But put on [or clothe yourselves with] the Lord Jesus Christ, and make no provision for the flesh, to fulfill its lusts" and Colossians 3:12-13: "Therefore, as the elect of God, holy and beloved, put on tender mercies, kindness, humility, meekness, longsuffering; bearing with one another, and forgiving one another, if anyone has a complaint against another; even as Christ forgave you, so you also must do."

There is another parable concerning a wedding in the Gospel accounts. This relates to the wedding banquet where the

---

[44] Revelation 19:7-8

king noticed someone not dressed in appropriate wedding apparel and arranged for him to be thrown out.[45] It was the custom in ancient Israel for the groom to provide simple garments for each of the wedding guests.[46] God likewise provides His born-again people with the unspoilt garments of salvation and the robe of righteousness[47] through the atoning work of Jesus upon the Cross. This is the initial eligibility to enter the wedding feast. To explore the wedding theme further, is it possible that there is a second stage of the sifting process for admittance to the marriage supper, depending on the amount of oil in the lamp of each virgin? Indeed, how else will we grow in sanctification without the ongoing ministry of the *Holy* Spirit in our lives? We are all commanded to be filled with the Spirit on a continual basis.[48] The tense of the Greek verb "to be filled" is a present tense implying being constantly being filled – such abiding in our Saviour will ensure the purity of our bridal garments. Ezekiel writes, "Behold, I shall judge between sheep and sheep."[49] Both wise and foolish virgins are all, in effect, sheep to be judged, a judgement for which we would be wise to prepare carefully.

---

[45] Matthew 22:11-14

[46] Bibletools.org "What the Bible says about Providing Wedding Garments for Guests" (from Forerunner Commentary)

[47] Isaiah 61:10

[48] Ephesians 5:18. (www.christianstudylibrary.org-Ephesians 5:18 "Be Filled with the Spirit")

[49] Ezekiel 34:17

Further Rapture passages in the New Testament

Apart from the parable of the wise and foolish virgins, does the Bible elsewhere suggest a Rapture of prepared believers only? The first passage to consider is: "'Many will say to Me in that day, 'Lord, Lord, have we not prophesied in Your name, cast out demons in Your name, and done many wonders in Your name?' And then I will declare to them, 'I never knew you; depart from Me, you who practice lawlessness!'"[50] Here, the Greek word for "knew" is the same one used to describe Mary's response when she was told she would have a child and asked how that could be as she *knew* no man. We understand that she is saying that she had no physical relationship with any man. The Hebrew word for "know" is *yada*, and the Aramaic word *yida* is similar. We see this word in the Old Testament. "Now Adam *knew* Eve his wife, and she conceived and bore Cain."[51] We can understand that the Lord is not looking for His people to do signs and wonders to qualify them to join Him at the wedding supper of the Lamb; He is looking for the few already in a close relationship with Him.

Another part of the New Testament to ponder upon is Luke 21:36: "Watch therefore, and pray always that you may be counted worthy [have strength] to escape all these things that will come to pass, and to stand before the Son of Man." We are instructed how to strengthen ourselves in the Lord in Jude

---

[50] Matthew 7:21-23. In this passage, "knew" derives from *ginosko*, a different Greek word to that used for "to know" in the wise and foolish virgins parable – *oida*. "The Parable of Ten Virgins" YouTube: Dr. Baruch Korman, loveisrael.org
[51] Genesis 4:1

1:20: "building yourselves up on your most holy faith, praying in the Holy Spirit." A great call to intimacy is found in the verse in Matthew 26:4 when Jesus wanted fellowship in the Garden of Gethsemane as He contemplated the agony ahead of Him, and found his disciples asleep: "What! Could you not watch with Me one hour?" We too can fellowship closely with the Lord in prayer as He is moved with compassion at what is ahead, both for His beloved people, Israel, and for the whole world during ever-increasing levels of birth pangs and tribulation.[52] Pray for Israel as they will soon face being surrounded by the Antichrist and the 10 horns of his kingdom.[53] Pray for salvation, for pastors and labourers to be equipped to help their people grow in becoming increasingly wise virgins and to not tolerate any worldly compromise in their lives.

The book of Revelation is our manual for the latter days. See how Jesus commends and make a special promise to the faithful, persevering church in Philadelphia, "'Because you have kept the word of My perseverance, I also will keep you from the hour of testing, that hour which is about to come upon the whole world, to test those who dwell on the earth.'"[54] Contrast this to the plea issued to the unresponsive, apathetic, lukewarm church, the church of Laodicea, considered by many to generally represent the Western end-times Church. "Behold, I stand at the door and knock. If anyone hears My voice and opens the door, I will come in to him and dine with him, and he with Me."[55] We see here the Lord pleading with His people

---

[52] As discussed in my book "Exploring the End Times and Interceding for Israel"
[53] Daniel 7:24, Revelation 17:12
[54] Revelation 3:10
[55] Revelation 3:20

to open their hearts to deep intimacy. To which group of end-times believers do we wish to spiritually identify? The faithful church which will be removed from the Tribulation, or those in the lukewarm, complacent church which needs instruction on how to enter into this close walk with the Lord to avoid the brutality of the Last Days before the return of Jesus?

What will the Tribulation be like?

This brings us on to the nature of the end-times Tribulation, which those close to the Lord will be removed from experiencing. We know that it will be a savage time, when Christians and Jews will be severely persecuted. We are told: "then they will deliver you up to tribulation and kill you, and you will be hated by all nations for My name's sake. And then many will be offended, will betray one another, and will hate one another. Then many false prophets will rise up and deceive many. And because lawlessness will abound, the love of many will grow cold. But he who endures to the end shall be saved."[56] The fifth seal of Revelation describes the souls under the altar who had been slain for the word of God and for their testimony.[57] It is not clear if this group is comprised only of those killed during the final seven years of this age, or whether it also includes the brave Christians who up to the Tribulation have daily been giving their lives for the Lord. Open Doors, a non-denominational mission supporting persecuted Christians

---

[56] Matthew 24:9-14
[57] Revelation 6:9

around the world, list on their website in July 2024 the countries where Christians face the most persecution. The list starts with North Korea, then Somalia, Libya, Eritrea, Yemen and Nigeria. They report that more believers are killed for their faith in Nigeria each year than everywhere else in the world combined. Shockingly, this level of persecution and murder of Christians is slated to severely escalate during the End Times.

The Scripture describes the martyrs of the fifth seal each being given a white robe and being told that they should rest for a little while "until both the number of their fellow servants and their brethren, who would be killed as they were, was completed."[58] We are told later, "Then I saw the souls of those who had been beheaded for their witness to Jesus and for the word of God, who had not worshiped the beast or his image, and had not received his mark on their foreheads or on their hands. And they lived and reigned with Christ for a thousand years."[59] The world will be led during the Tribulation by the Antichrist, who will orchestrate this savagery against believers in the Lord Jesus. This group of the Christians who are persecuted unto death will, in my opinion, comprise both those who are not taken in the Rapture and also those who subsequently come to faith – providing both groups refuse the Mark of the Beast and do not worship the beast, the Antichrist. Note, and be encouraged, how these believers will be rewarded by ruling and reigning with the Messiah for 1,000 years.

Even though the Rapture will, in my understanding, happen some years before the Second Coming, nevertheless this does

---

[58] Revelation 6:11
[59] Revelation 20:4

not preclude faithful Christians having to live through tough times, for which we would also be wise to prepare. The four horses of the Apocalypse comprise the first four seals in chapter 6 of the book of Revelation. These horses probably start riding out after the Rapture, at the start of the last seven years of this age, also known as the 70th week of Daniel. Nevertheless, prior to the snatching away, we are all being increasingly impacted by the ever-intensifying labour pains or birth pangs coming upon the earth.[60] All of us, whether wisely prepared for the Rapture, or not, may shortly be encountering very difficult times.

How will Christians fare during the Tribulation?

What will Christians left behind be facing after the Rapture of the church? We have touched on the distressing matter of the beheading of believers at that time. To illustrate how the details may work out, you may be interested in two dreams of the Tribulation available on YouTube. The first is a detailed account by the late Ken Peters, which he presented to the Prophecy Club in the year 2000, describing the dream he had 20 years previously: "I Saw The Tribulation (Full Version) Ken Peters."[61] The second is complementary, exploring different areas, and entitled "Jesus took me to the Tribulation and gave me a glimpse of what's to come. I had this visitation 2014: Last

[60] Matthew 24:8 and Mark 13:8
[61] https://www.youtube.com/watch?v=VOo5yvo3hHI&t=6668s

Days, Brandon Biggs."[62]   These dreams appear to illustrate many verses in the Bible. For example, we see the fulfilment of Luke 13:22-28: "But many who are first will be last, and the last, first," in the order in which believers are taken to heaven. We hear of individual Christian pastors, and television ministers left behind after the Rapture to face angry church members, who wanted to kill these men because of their failure to warn about what was to come and prepare their people. We can picture the humble devout church attendee being raptured and taken to heaven before some leaders who had been compromised in their walk with God, despite their high-profile ministries. These foolish virgins will have to persevere here on earth during the Tribulation before they can enter heaven. The dreams describe the mass panic and hysteria following the removal of the Christians and children in the Rapture and how this will in turn be attributed to alien abduction. It is suggested that this very atmosphere of chaos and deep fear, causing a breakdown in law and order, gives rise to the Islamic Antichrist coming to power, offering order, strong leadership and peace to those who follow him. We are told he will demand worship on a Friday and that people take his electronic mark in order to access towns where there will be food. If the mark is refused then no mercy is shown; the consequence is instant decapitation. We learn how the Islamic world will welcome the Antichrist as their messiah, the Mahdi.[63] We hear of siblings

[62] https://www.youtube.com/watch?v=RlS3QooVBxg&t=830s
[63] For full details of the meaning and implications of this term, see Joel Richardson's book, "The Islamic Antichrist." 2009. Chapter 4, "The Mahdi: Islam's Awaited Messiah." PDF available to read free of charge on the internet at joelstrumpet.com/wp- content/uploads/2019/02/Islamic-Antichrist.pdf   Also, see Nelson's Walters YouTube video: "Muslim Jesus and Christian Jesus are Both Coming

born during the Tribulation reaching an age when they could talk. We hear details about the "foul and loathsome sore [which] came upon the men who had the Mark of the Beast and those who worshiped his image."[64] Both men report seeing the Antichrist being worshipped on large screens, which is interesting in light of the verse: "If anyone worships the beast *and its image*, and receives its mark on his forehead or on his hand..."[65] (author's emphasis). We hear how the Antichrist will be a Gentile. We already know this because we are told in Revelation 13:1 how he rises up from the sea – a Scriptural term for the nations. By contrast, Revelation explains that the False Prophet comes out of the earth, a synonym for Israel.[66] Indeed a name of a specific Israeli is suggested for the False Prophet. We are also given clues as to how some Christians will be drawn into this one-world religious system.

Please note that it is the responsibility of the bride to prepare *herself* for her own wedding; she cannot leave it all to the bridegroom. We are each responsible to get ourselves ready for the Rapture that will unite us with our heavenly Bridegroom. In addition, we cannot prepare anyone else, although we should be praying and encouraging others to see the importance of this spiritual preparation. At the very least, if we find ourselves discussing the Last Days, we should warn of the world being taken over by the Antichrist, supported by militant Islamic groups. Picture door-to-door visits to find anyone sheltering

---

Back - Which One Will Churches Follow?"
www.youtube.com/watch?v=2ozP7YTl1RY
[64] Revelation 16:2
[65] Revelation 14:9
[66] Revelation 13:11

within who has not taken the Mark of the Beast! Fail on a Friday to worship the Antichrist, or hide a Bible on the property? All such *offences* will carry the barbaric punishment of decapitation! Imagine turning on the radio and instead of music, out blares Islamic doctrine and calls to prayer, professionally delivered in BBC-style received pronunciation. Envisage the hardships of Christians fleeing persecution and having to leave the comfort of their own homes.

At the time of writing, there is serious civil unrest among people groups in the United Kingdom. This is the sort of situation to which Jesus refers when He warns that nation will rise against nation.[67] The Greek word used here for nation is *ethnos*, meaning people group rather than a country in the geographical sense.[68] This tragic and seemingly intractable situation moves us to intercede for revival. It is an opportunity to share the gospel of salvation. Our views on the soon-return of Jesus, the Rapture and the Tribulation may provide an apt introduction to the subject. One term for this is "apocalyptic evangelism." Understanding how eschatology is unfolding helps to equip us with feet shod with the preparation of the gospel of peace.[69] Perhaps too, it will provide us with new angles to speak to those who have fallen away from the Faith. "Deliver those who are drawn toward death, and hold back those stumbling to the slaughter."[70] The Apostle James tells us

---

[67] Matthew 24:7
[68] Bible Tools.org: "What the Bible says about Ethnos" (From Forerunner Commentary)
[69] Ephesians 6:15
[70] Proverbs 24:11

that mercy triumphs over judgement,[71] and we can cry out on behalf of the lost, claiming this truth.

Testing the spirits

We need to exercise prayerful, godly discernment in assessing the authenticity and reliability of these dreams. We have to judge such things by the plumb line of the Word of God. We are instructed that: "the testimony of Jesus is the spirit of prophecy."[72] We understand that there will be a great outpouring of the Holy Spirit in the last day: "I will pour out My Spirit on all flesh; your sons and your daughters shall prophesy, your old men shall dream dreams, your young men shall see visions."[73] We are exhorted to "hear what the Spirit says to the churches"[74] and warned, "Beloved, do not believe every spirit, but test the spirits, whether they are of God; because many false prophets have gone out into the world."[75] We need to assess what is presented with the attitude described in 1 Thessalonians 5:19- 21, "Do not quench the Spirit. Do not despise prophecies. Test all things; hold fast what is good." We also should appreciate the broad similarity in these two parallel dreams, as we are instructed, "by the mouth of two or three witnesses every word may be established."[76] Even if you are

[71] James 2:13
[72] Revelation 19:10
[73] Joel 2:28
[74] Revelation 2:7
[75] 1 John 4:1
[76] Matthew 18:16

among the sceptical, I would encourage you to watch the two presentations. Ponder upon whether there is a witness in your spirit to their validity, or if they fit into the category described by the prophet Jeremiah, those who "prophesy to you a false vision, divination, a worthless thing, and the deceit of their heart."[77] This discernment is vital as the return of the Bridegroom fast approaches. When the disciples asked Jesus for the signs of His coming, His first response was to instruct them to be wary of deception.[78] We are warned to avoid false teachers by Paul, those who: "... teach otherwise, and consent not to wholesome words, *even* the words of our Lord Jesus Christ, and to the doctrine which is according to godliness."[79]

The Seven Churches of the Book of Revelation

The most popular view of the wise and foolish virgins is to interpret the foolish as unsaved nominal Christians – the tares (weeds) among the wheat.[80] However, it is worth considering the parable in the light of the letters to the seven churches in Revelation 2 and 3. Although these churches may, broadly speaking, represent different churches over the course of history, it is instructive to learn what God is saying to us today through these letters.[81] Presently, here in the West, the established churches tend to be lukewarm and therefore Laodicean,

---

[77] Jeremiah 14:14
[78] Matthew 24:4
[79] 1 Timothy 6:3-5
[80] Matthew 13:24-30
[81] Got Questions website "Seven Churches."

yet we recognise that in other parts of the world the end-times church may be more like Smyrna, suffering persecution. Other churches in these days have lost their first love like Ephesus, and so on. Twice Jesus tells the churches that He strongly objects to the deeds of the Nicolaitans, which He likens to the teaching of Balaam that caused the Israelites to eat food sacrificed to idols and to commit sexual immorality.[82] The origin of the Nicolaitans is believed to be Nicolas from Antioch who was chosen to be one of the deacons in the early church in Jerusalem.[83] Nicolas was a spiritual compromiser, teaching that Christians could combine paganism with their faith in Christ. Irenaeus, Tertullian, and Clement of Alexandria attest to the existence of the Nicolaitans in the second century.[84] The Pulpit Commentary explains that the view of the Nicolaitans was that those who have been made free in Christ could not be harmed by idolatry and sensuality. On the contrary, Jesus does not want His people living in compromise, and this is a challenge for us to meditate upon if we want to be among the wise virgins.

Each of the seven churches in Revelation is told of a reward if they overcome.[85] Special privileges are promised to the overcomers, ranging from being given authority over the nations in the millennial kingdom, to being guaranteed to never have their name blotted out of the Book of Life.[86] This is such a challenge for each of us seeking to be wise virgins: to overcome the areas of oppression and sin in our individual walk

---

[82] Revelation 2:6, 14-16
[83] Internet article of RENNER Ministries and Acts 6:5
[84] Ellicott's Commentary for English Readers
[85] Revelation 2:7,11,17,26 and 3:5,12,21
[86] Revelation 2:26, 3:5

ranging from bitterness to jealously to self-pity to greed and all kinds of uncleanness. This is an ugly and ill-fitting robe to wear for those aspiring to be wise virgins in these Last Days. Our prayer should be, "Search me, O God, and know my heart; try me, and know my anxieties; and see if there is any wicked way in me, and lead me in the way everlasting."[87] This concept of overcoming is a very important one to remember. As we seek to draw closer to the Lord, we may become aware of circumstances, our old nature, or our spiritual enemy threatening to trip us up in our walk of faith. These discouraging obstacles in our pathway should be viewed as challenges to overcome, rather than an excuse to give up. "I discipline my body and bring it into subjection, lest, when I have preached to others, I myself should become disqualified."[88] We are exhorted to discard every encumbrance, and the sin which so easily ensnares or entangles us, and to run with endurance the race that lies before us.[89]

What will happen to the unwise virgins? It appears from the letters to the seven churches that they are not assured of the various blessings promised to the overcomers. Is this because they will be vulnerable to scuppering their salvation through taking the Mark of the Beast out of fear for their lives? It is possible for believers to make a shipwreck of their faith.[90] We are assured that those who persevere to the end will be saved.[91] Jesus instructs us that there will be weeping and gnashing of teeth at the end of this age when the unsaved realise that they

[87] Psalm 139:23-24
[88] 1 Corinthians 9:26-27
[89] Hebrews 12:1
[90] 1 Timothy 1:19
[91] Matthew 24:13

are consigned to everlasting punishment.[92] Similar extreme expressions of anguish and anger can be expected among the foolish virgins to whom the door to the marriage supper of the Lamb will have been shut at the Rapture.

We may want to search the Scriptures for clues as to the fate of the unwise virgins who enter the Tribulation and subsequently repent. They did not overcome before the Rapture, thereby excluding themselves. However, for those ones who return to and keep the Faith, enduring until the end, overcoming by the blood of the Lamb and by the word of their testimony, loving not their lives even unto death,[93] what will be their reward? Will they share in the promises made to the overcomers who qualify for the Rapture in Revelation chapters 2 and 3? What will their role be in the Millennium and in the eternal state? Will they be honoured in a special way for their courage in living for the Lord in light of almost-certain martyrdom? Will they be among those referred to in James 1:12 who, having persevered under trial, are going to receive the crown of life? How many of them will be among the glorious group shown to the Apostle John in heaven, "the ones who come out of the great tribulation, and washed their robes and made them white in the blood of the Lamb,"[94] those who will be honoured with the role of serving God day and night in His temple? In the apostle's apocalyptic vision, he saw those who prevailed over the beast, its image, its mark and the number of its name. These overcomers were standing, holding harps, on the heavenly sea of glass. An immense privilege was granted

---

[92] Matthew 13:42,50
[93] Revelation 12:11
[94] Revelation 7:14

to them: "They sing the song of Moses, the servant of God, and the song of the Lamb, saying: "Great and marvelous are Your works, Lord God Almighty! Just and true are Your ways, O King of the saints!"[95]

Why a pre-tribulation Rapture?

Augustine also said, "In essentials, unity; in non-essentials, liberty; in all things, charity." Theology of the fundamentals of the Faith is of vital importance to a Christian. We need to be firm and unwavering concerning doctrines such as the Trinity, the divine nature of the Son, and the infallibility of the Word of God. However, there are secondary complex and mysterious issues of a theological nature upon which godly, well-respected theologians and teachers disagree, and even may change their minds about in time. In these matters, we need to exercise tolerance and forbearance, in a spirit of love, one towards another. This is the case with eschatology (the study of End Times), including the Rapture. It is prudent to hold our views about such a subject lightly and with humility, since we are instructed by the Lord that He will destroy the wisdom of the wise and put to one side the cleverness of the clever.[96]

Scripture assures us that the wrath of God is not the heritage of His children. This is made clear in 1 Thessalonians 5:9: "For God did not appoint us to wrath, but to obtain salvation through our Lord Jesus Christ." Then, in Romans 5:9, "Much

---

[95] Revelation 15:2-3
[96] 1 Corinthians 1:19

more then, having now been justified by His blood, we shall be saved from wrath through Him." We have already looked at the promise to the faithful church of Philadelphia to be kept from the hour of testing.[97] These verses rule out the post-tribulation rapture view, because that would be *after* the wrath of God is poured out following the sixth seal of Revelation 6, when men call out to be hidden from the Lord and His coming wrath.[98] Those verses support either a pre-tribulation or a pre-wrath understanding, because they allow for a Rapture before the wrath of God. A pre-wrath Rapture view would place the Rapture at or before the sixth seal, arguably a year and 10 days before the Second Coming.[99]

Why then should we expect a Rapture a whole seven years before the End of the Age, the traditional pre-tribulation view? To answer this question, we have to consider the 70-week prophetic outline of the End Times given to Daniel about Israel,[100] which is explained on the helpful website Got Questions.[101] I have also described it in my book, "Exploring the End Times and Interceding for Israel." 69 weeks of years are announced to Israel from the decree to rebuild Jerusalem until the vicarious death of the Messiah. Then there is a gap of unspecified length before the final "week," meaning seven years. The Church is not mentioned in this 70-week prophecy. Now we know that the Christian church started immediately after the

---

[97] Revelation 3:10
[98] Revelation 6:16-17
[99] Nelson Walters YouTube teaching video "Noah's Flood and End Time Prophecy." www.youtube.com/watch?v=aYUT8gvqp-Y
[100] Daniel 9:24-27
[101] "What are the seventy weeks of Daniel?" https://www.gotquestions.org/seventy-weeks.html

crucifixion of the Lord Jesus, when the 69th week was completed. It may therefore be assumed that the Church will disappear from the picture just before the start of the final seven years, when the countdown to the 70th week starts again. The other complementary assumption in the pre-tribulation framework is that because the word 'church' is not used in the book of Revelation after chapter 3, the Church age must be completed by this point. Hence, it is surmised that when John hears a voice "like a trumpet speaking ... saying, 'come up here,'"[102] this represents the Rapture of the Church before the seal, bowl and trumpet judgements subsequently described in the book of Revelation. The trumpet-like voice he hears is likened to the sound to which Paul refers in his description of the Rapture: "For the trumpet will sound, and the dead will be raised incorruptible, and we shall be changed."[103] As previously mentioned, each of the Rapture views has its problems and these three assumptions, which include arguments from silence, are a weakness of this view, known as classical premillennial dispensationalism. On the positive side, we are told to look forward to our blessed hope,[104] that Jesus is coming when we do not expect Him.[105] As before the days of Noah, there will be people at ease – eating, drinking and giving in marriage prior to His coming.[106] These verses favour a pre-tribulation view rather than one that puts His return at a particular specified identifiable point during the harrowing events prophesied in

---

[102] Revelation 4:1
[103] 1 Corinthians 15:52
[104] Titus 2:13
[105] Matthew 24:44
[106] Matthew 24:37-39

the book of Revelation. That is a weakness in both the pre-wrath and post-tribulation theories.

We may wonder what is the purpose of a pre-tribulation Rapture. Clearly, the whole world would be suddenly plunged into an apocalyptic scene following the departure of Christians. Everyone will be aware of the awful change in the spiritual atmosphere once the restrainer is removed, and looting, chaos and every kind of evil and crime explodes. There will be farms, factories, health facilities, supermarkets and transport hubs instantly short-staffed. The supply chains of food, fuel, spare parts and other necessities will be devastated and will urgently require fixing. The overriding emotions will be fear and panic. Envision the trauma of those who witness graves opening in a cemetery and glorified bodies rising![107] Consider how astonished people will be when they see their work colleagues suddenly drawn up to heaven![108] The urgent need will be to find someone to bring structure to this alarming new world, a strong charismatic leader who will impose law and order and project a persona of peace. Enter the Antichrist! He will even appear to solve the unrest in the Middle East by sanctioning the rebuilding of the Jewish Temple in Jerusalem, possibly making use of the space on the Temple Mount between the Dome of the Rock Islamic shrine and the Al Aqsa mosque. We can only speculate on what Israel will need to do in return for this false peace; presumably, give up yet more land.

People of every nation and every geographical area will be asking questions about how and why this dire calamity has happened over the entire globe. We can safely say that children

---

[107] 1 Thessalonians 4:26
[108] Matthew 24:40-41

of Christian families will be taken, because of the Scripture which asserts that the children of believers are holy.[109] Tim LaHaye (in his Left Behind series)[110] suggested that young children from unbelieving families, all over the world, will also be raptured. This is a reasonable speculation because Jesus says, "Let the little children come to Me, and do not forbid them; for of such is the kingdom of heaven."[111] This shocking event will be devastating, and it follows that some will try and heal their wounds by having children once again. The task of bringing them up in this new world order will be grim, especially for those families who refuse the Mark of the Beast and seek to hide from the authorities. The Lord is merciful, not wishing any to perish but for all to be saved.[112] He will send an angel with the everlasting Gospel to share with every tribe, nation, language and people.[113] We can expect that in their distress and perplexity, given the supernatural context, that this angel will have the attention of those who hear, provided that they have not hardened their hearts. It is amazing that the first gospel message given by the exuberant apostles in Acts 2, was heard by Jewish listeners from different nations each in their own tongue![114] When the angel delivers the words of the final gospel message of this age, we can likewise expect people from all over the world to hear it in their native language. This will be the ultimate fulfilment of Jesus' prediction, "this gospel of the kingdom will be preached in all the world as a witness to all

---

[109] 1 Corinthians 7:14
[110] Tyndale House Publishing
[111] Matthew 19:14
[112] 2 Peter 3:9
[113] Revelation 14:6
[114] Acts 2:1-13

the nations, and then the end will come."[115] This will be the very last harvest of souls for the kingdom of God. It will be followed by an entirely different and sobering harvest of the entire globe; "so the angel swung his sickle over the earth and gathered the grapes of the earth, and he threw them into the great winepress of God's wrath."[116]

We have already alluded to a pre-tribulation Rapture providing plenty of time for backslidden Christians and prodigals to repent, to lead many to salvation, to teach about God's plans for the End of the Age, and to lead groups of new believers. A Tribulation immediately before or after the outpouring of the wrath of God would surely fail to provide this same opportunity for reflection, repentance, redemption and reward.

The apostle Paul teaches us that salvation has come to the Gentiles to provoke Israel to jealousy.[117] Could a pre-tribulation Rapture of mainly Gentiles play a part in making Jewish people jealous? Inevitably, the rabbis will be consulted to provide an answer to the mystery of what has happened in the sudden disappearance of so many. The most likely reply is that this event includes a divine punishment of Jewish believers for being traitors to their Jewish heritage by following Jesus. How many will find that convincing in the light of this event being worldwide and embracing all people groups? The remaining Jewish people will be devastated, frightened, and confused at the sudden departure of countless individuals. They will know that, wherever the Messianic believers have gone, they are together with their young children, and out of the way of a most

---

[115] Matthew 24:14
[116] Revelation 14:19
[117] Romans 11:11

perilous situation. Perhaps as the days get darker, some will wonder if these families are in the safety and joy of heaven. This will indeed provoke some to jealousy. There will be plenty of time to ponder and search for answers: seven years. The first half of this period, before the Antichrist desecrates the Temple in Jerusalem, may superficially appear to be peaceful as regards the borders in the Land of Israel. It is the second half, the remaining three-and-a-half years, which is known as "The Time of Jacob's Trouble" or the "Great Tribulation." Tragically, during the second half of the final week of Daniel, two-thirds of those in Israel will die.[118] The horrifying post-rapture situation will speak deeply to those who have Messianic family members, friends, neighbours and colleagues who had tried to reach out to them with the Gospel in the past. There are sadly some among the Jewish community in Israel and in the rest of the world who despise Christians inwardly – even their hearts of stone may start to soften. Ezekiel writes that God will replace stony hearts with hearts of flesh.[119] The ultimate fulfilment of this will be at the Second Coming when the people of Israel look on Him whom they pierced and mourn bitterly.[120] This is the point at which all surviving Israel will be saved.

---

[118] Zechariah 13:8
[119] Ezekiel 36:26
[120] Zechariah 12:10

Some further theological considerations

You may be struck by how my understanding of the wise and foolish virgins and the Rapture combines both the classic pre-tribulation and the post-tribulation views. Some Christians will be delivered and translated to the safety of heaven before the dark night of the Tribulation, and others will need to persevere through the fire of affliction unto death or the Second Coming of the Lord Jesus at the end of the age. This approach also helps answer inevitable questions, such as the reason why there are so many instructions for believers during the Tribulation. One such passage concerns what the Jewish people should do when they see the Antichrist desecrating the temple in Jerusalem.[121] If all the Bible believers are taken, then who remains to apply the Scriptures to matters of salvation, discipleship and navigation through the final week of Daniel? However, if backslidden Christians, including some Bible teachers and ministers, are left here on earth because they were not considered worthy to be included in the Rapture of the Church, then they will know exactly what is going to happen. They would be highly motivated and equipped, if they turn back to the Lord, to prepare others, including those whom they lead to the Lord at that time.

The partial Rapture theory is believed to have been developed by Robert Govett MA (Oxon) (1813-1901). He was a former Anglican turned non-denominational pastor and theologian with a reputation for having brilliant intellectual and analytical capabilities. He founded Surrey Chapel, Norwich, in 1854. Charles Hadden Spurgeon commented that Robert

---

[121] Mark 13:14

Govett was writing 100 years before his time and that, in the future, his work would be highly treasured.[122] Govett took the view that the Rapture is for the watchful, consigning the remainder of believers to the Day of Trouble. He made much of the analogy to which Jesus refers concerning the days of Noah,[123] and took the view that there will be several Raptures.[124] His writings are still available, including "The Parable of the Ten Virgins" and "The Saints' Rapture."[125] Robert Govett was succeeded at Surrey Chapel by D.M. Panton, B.A. (Cantab.) (1870-1955) who also adhered to a partial Rapture perspective and promoted this teaching as editor in "The Dawn (London)," where writers such as Ira E. David, Sarah Foulkes Moore, William Leask and C.G.A. Gibson-Smith contributed articles in support.[126] Other proponents of a partial Rapture include the British Brethren Bible teacher G.H. Lang (1874-1958), G.H. Pember (1837-1910), the English theologian and author affiliated with the Plymouth Brethren,[127] and Joseph Seiss (1823-1904), the American theologian and Lutheran minister. The Canadian interdenominational minister

[122] www.themillennialkingdom.org.uk "ROBERT GOVETT, M. A."
[123] Matthew 24:36-39
[124] For details of his view see his article reproduced on www.watchman-nee.nl/partial.htm: "Unwatchful believers of the Church will be left in the Great Tribulation."
[125] www.icmbooksdirect.co.uk
[126] www.raptureofchurch.com/Eschatology/4.htm
[127] www.myrtlefieldhouse.com. "Some observations on the doctrine called 'Partial Rapturism' or 'Conditional Kingdom'" and www.brethrenarchive.org

Albert Benjamin Simpson (1843-1919) gave serious consideration to the doctrine.[128] Watchman Nee (1903-1972), the Chinese church leader, likened the Rapture to a harvest where only the ripe crops (mature believers) are gathered. He believed that most Christians would require the process of the Tribulation in order to "ripen" and become mature overcomers.[129] A selective Rapture has always been a minority view over the centuries of church history. However, that is no reason to dismiss it as being without merit. We already understand that "... narrow *is* the gate and difficult *is* the way which leads to life, and there are few who find it."[130]

The emphasis of Jesus' teachings in the Olivet Discourse[131] is on being *ready* for the Rapture. Believers who are interested in the End Times will have different attitudes on what it means to prepare. Many in the pre-tribulation camp eagerly focus on monitoring the various signs such as the situation in Israel, as well as global earthquakes, pestilences, and wars. Those with a mid-tribulation, pre-wrath or post-tribulation view may well be particularly interested in personal practical preparation for the dark days ahead. Surely, whatever our conviction on the timing of the Rapture, we should all be directing our energy to growing in holiness. Theological terms can be very off-putting. Perhaps the best term for the view here being presented is "Bridegroom readiness!" John the Baptist understood this role of the Messiah and so told his own disciples: "He who has the

[128] prophecycountdown.com/wp-content/uploads/2009/09/Oil-In-Your-Vessel1.pdf
[129] www.watchmannee.org/scriptural-teachings.html section on Rapture
[130] Matthew 7:14
[131] Matthew 24 and 25

bride is the bridegroom; but the friend of the bridegroom, who stands and hears him, rejoices greatly because of the bridegroom's voice."[132]

This leads us to consider other ways in which this writing may jar with the theology of some. The idea of a level of conditionality for Christians to be admitted to the marriage supper of the Lamb cuts across standard pre-tribulation doctrine, which tends to view the foolish virgins as those who were never truly the Lord's. The foolish are considered as those only able to briefly light a dry wick because they never had any oil in their vessels to start with.[133] The pre-tribulation theologian and Bible teacher, John F. Walvoord, presents a staunch rebuttal of the concept of a partial Rapture, which he describes as "heterodox," meaning that it is not the generally accepted view of pre-tribulationists. One of his main objections is that just as salvation is not by works, neither is the consequential benefit of salvation, the Rapture.[134] Dr Thomas Ice, Executive Director of The Pre-Trib Research Center, amusingly writes that even those Christians not expecting the Rapture, and who have to be taken "kicking and screaming," will nevertheless be taken![135] He also quotes Randolph Yeager,[136] who wittily remarked that a partial *rapture* seems to imply *rupture* in the Body of Christ. The Lord wants us to be alert and watchful, looking forward to the Rapture: "Watch therefore, for you know nei-

---

[132] John 3:29
[133] www.ccel.org/ccel/edersheim/lifetimes.x.vii.html
[134] walvoord.com/article/63
[135] www.rapture-notes.com/wise-and-foolish-virgins
[136] American theologian, former University professor and author of such books as "The Renaissance New Testament."

ther the day nor the hour in which the Son of Man is coming."[137] Is it possible that some Christians who fail to heed this
advice, rather than being taken "kicking and screaming," could
be overlooked and miss the marriage supper? "Blessed *are*
those servants whom the master, when he comes, will find
watching. Assuredly, I say to you that he will gird himself and
have them sit down *to eat,* and will come and serve them."[138]
When Jesus comes to collect His bride for the marriage supper, surely He is looking for watchful believers who enjoy
spending time in His presence. If this is the case, then the result would indeed lead to the *rupture* of the church alluded to
by Randolph Yeager.

A simple internet search will reveal a string of names of
Christian leaders, teachers and well-known personalities, who
have over the last five years or so, spectacularly fallen from
grace into repugnant sin.[139] We may even be personally ac-
quainted with Christian leaders who are habitually unholy in
conduct or speech or abusive towards their flock. This sad
state of affairs surely cannot be explained by the excuse that
none of these individuals were ever truly the Lord's, that they
never belonged to Him and never experienced the oil of the
Holy Spirit. It is more likely that they are "foolish virgins."
While we were bringing up our three sons, my late mother-in-
law used to wisely say that some children learn the easy way,
whilst others learn the hard way. How true this will be for

---

[137] Matthew 25:13

[138] Luke 12:37

[139] For example, "A respected Christian leader has been caught in serious sin. Now what?" Premier Christianity Magazine 3rd October 2022
and "Church Leadership Scandals and the Miracle of Ordinary Faithful-
ness" Firebrand Magazine June 25th 2024

prodigals and backsliders who enter the Tribulation, but subsequently cry out to the Lord for His salvation and mercy, purpose not to take the Mark of the Beast, and are willing to lay
down their lives for the Faith.

The parable of the prodigal son and the father who waits for
his return[140] gives us every reason to hope, intercede and believe for the prodigals to return to His sheepfold, even if they
do not make the Rapture. There are two situations whereby
Christians clearly will irretrievably lose their salvation. Firstly,
those who publicly deny the Faith as a consequence of their
backsliding and unbelief,[141] and, secondly, those who take the
Mark of the Beast.[142] However, there is hope for foolish virgins
who have let the Lord down and consequently miss the Rapture. When considering this subject and our personal assur-
ance of salvation, we can rely on verses like, "I give them eternal life, and they shall never perish; neither shall anyone snatch
them out of My hand,"[143] and, "the one who comes to Me I
will by no means cast out."[144] Surely, we are safely held in the
hands of our Good Shepherd, yet we are free to make the
choice to step out of the sheepfold and, subsequently, if we do
not harden our hearts nor take the Mark of the Beast, we can
step back in genuine repentance by the bountiful grace of God.
Consider what Daniel describes and how this will apply to
those who backslide and miss the Rapture: "And some of
those of understanding shall fall, to refine them, purify them,

---

140 Luke 15:11-32
141 Hebrews 6:4-6
142 Revelation 20:4
143 John 10:28
144 John 6:37

and make them white, until the time of the end; because it is still for the appointed time."[145]

In biblical times there were two types of sheep pens. There was the large public sort in a city or village which could accommodate more than one flock at a time. This was protected by a gatekeeper and the shepherd would call his own sheep, who would respond and come out because they recognised his voice. Then out in the rural areas, there would have been rough sheep pens built from piles of stones with a gap in the makeshift wall to enable the sheep to come in and out. At night in the countryside, the shepherd would sleep across the entrance and he would literally be the human door.[146] Any thief who wanted to snatch the valuable sheep would have to go through the barrier of the shepherd. This is the background to Jesus describing Himself as the door (or gate) in John 10. No one can snatch us away because He is protecting His sheep.

Next, we come to the objection that the gifts of the Spirit such as prophecy ceased after the completion of the New Testament. Does this presentation offend those who hold to cessationism? Indeed it may, since it alludes to prophetic dreams. Many will be familiar with the arguments of those who contend for cessationism, and may well be persuaded by them.[147] Paul instructs us in 1 Corinthians 13 that prophecies will cease (v8), and also, "... we know in part and we prophesy in part. But when that which is perfect has come, then that which is in

---

[145] Daniel 11:35

[146] Got Questions Internet article: "What did Jesus mean when He said 'I am the door?' (John 10:7)?"

[147] A good outline is provided in the internet article "Got Questions – Is cessationism biblical? What is a cessationist?"

part will be done away."[148] Each of us has to decide what is meant by "that which is perfect." There is a sharp debate in the Christian community on this subject. On one side we have cessationists who believe that prophecies ceased when the canon of Scripture was completed. Then, we have continuationists who axiomatically believe that such gifts continue until the end of the age. If the perfect is marked by the completion of all the books in the Bible, then it follows that Paul's writing about the gifts of the Spirit in the previous chapter was only intended to hold true for a relatively short period of time. There is nothing to indicate this in the Scriptures.[149] On the contrary, if the perfect is the return and rule of the Lord Jesus, this fits much better with the Old Testament prophecy about God pouring out His Spirit on all people in the Day of the Lord, old men dreaming dreams and young men seeing visions.[150] The American revivalist Jonathan Edwards witnessed notable manifestations of the Holy Spirit in the First and Second Great Awakenings in the 1730s and 1740s.[151] George Whitefield (1714-1770) claimed to receive fresh teachings and communications daily from the Holy Spirit. He attributed the very words that he preached to the Holy Spirit and maintained that it was thus unnecessary to prepare what he was to say. His first sermon was so powerful that it is said that it drove 15

---

[148] 1 Corinthians 13:9-10

[149] Chris Reed, Brandon Biggs: "Where are we on God's prophetic time clock?" YouTube Last Days. See too www.samstorms.org "Does the Existence of a Completed Canon of Scripture Preclude the Need for Signs, Wonders, and Miracles" and "Does Cessationism Still Stand? A Response to Tom Pennington"

[150] Joel 2:28

[151] lexloiz.wordpress.com "Jonathan Edwards Defends the Effects of the Power of the Spirit"

people mad![152] If we are praying for revival in these perilous
End Times, we should be expecting even greater outpourings
of the Holy Spirit. Yet more oil for our lamps!

We are now moving on to consider whether paying attention
to dreams and visions is somehow unspiritual and of the flesh,
cutting across the strict warning: "Do not add to His words,
lest He rebuke you, and you be found a liar."[153] Regarding the
words contained in the book of Revelation, we are also told:
"If anyone adds to them, God will add to him the plagues described in this book. And if anyone takes away from the words
of this book of prophecy, God will take away his share in the
tree of life and the holy city, which are described in this
book."[154] Two different Greek words used in the original New
Testament text both translate as "word" in English. *Logos* is
the word used for the unchanging written Word of God, the
Holy Bible, the final authority in all matters of faith and conduct. It occurs in the warning we have just looked at in Revelation, besides other verses in the New Testament.[155] Nevertheless, when Jesus quotes from Deuteronomy: "Man shall not
live by bread alone, but by every word that proceeds from the
mouth of God,"[156] the Greek word used in the text is not *logos*

---

[152] "Refreshings of God's Spirit in My Soul: George Whitefield and the
Role of the Holy Spirit in Preaching" Frankie Melton, Jr
[153] Proverbs 30:6
[154] Revelation 22:19
[155] Luke 8:11, John 1:1,14 , 6:60, 17:17, Philippians 2:16, Hebrews 4:12
[156] Matthew 4:4

but *rhema*. This term *rhema* refers to the spoken word and oc-curs in other New Testament verses too.[157] So, should we con-fine ourselves to the reliable *logos* Word, or could the Holy Spirit possibly give us further enlightenment through certain *rhema* dreams and visions, providing that they do not contra-dict the written *logos*? It is my opinion, for reasons I will ex-plain, that authentic dreams and visions from the Lord may well be playing a part in the progressive revelation in these Last Days.

The prophet Daniel was told: "... shut up the words, and seal the book until the time of the end; many shall run to and fro, and knowledge shall increase."[158] In these Last Days, people are increasingly poring over the book of Daniel, their eyes run-ning over the text and gaining further insight into its meaning. The Apostles were told by the risen Lord Jesus that it was not for them to know the times, nor the seasons, which the Father had fixed by His own authority.[159] However, we are no longer in that position. Israel, the fig tree, blossomed in 1948,[160] her-alding the season of the fast-approaching Second Coming. I believe that God Himself is sending dreams and visions in these days to unseal and clarify biblical prophecy, increasing knowledge of the End Times and preparing His people for what is shortly ahead. We are instructed in the Gospel of John that the Holy Spirit will tell us things to come.[161] Many of us

---

[157] Luke 1:38, John 6:63,68, Acts 11:16, Romans 10:8-9,17, Ephesians 5:26, 6:17, 1 Peter 1:25, Hebrews 11:3
[158] Daniel 12:4
[159] Acts 1:7
[160] Matthew 24:32-33. Israel's declaration of independence took place on 14th May 1948.
[161] John 16:13

have read the fine book by Corrie ten Boom, "The Hiding Place."[162] Corrie recalls a conversation when her father taught her that God will give His children the grace to face death exactly when they need it, in just the same way that he only gave his young daughter her train ticket moments before they boarded a train. Are the dreams and visions referred to part of the heavenly ticket many of us need before the sudden arrival and instantaneous departure of the "train" of the Rapture?

In ancient times, it was accepted that God speaks to men through dreams. In Job, the oldest book of the Bible, Elihu, one of Job's would-be comforters states, "For God may speak in one way, or in another, yet man does not perceive it. In a dream, in a vision of the night, when deep sleep falls upon men, while slumbering on their beds."[163] In Genesis 41, we read of Joseph interpreting Pharoah's dream of seven years of abundance followed by seven years of famine. This led to Joseph being in a position to save the family of his father Jacob, also known as Israel, from starvation in the land of Canaan. In the book of Daniel, Nebuchadnezzar demanded an accurate interpretation of his dream concerning the statue with a head of gold.[164] If a later Joseph, the foster-father of Jesus, had disregarded the dreams he was given, he would not have married Mary, the mother of the Messiah, and the young Child would have been murdered, along with the other innocents below the age of two.[165]

---

[162] Hodder & Stoughton edition published 2004
[163] Job 33:14-15
[164] Daniel 2
[165] Matthew 1:20-21, 2:13,19

Why should we pay attention in this day and age to contemporary dreams and visions? We already are blessed with a multitude of high quality online biblical teachings, not to mention access to a rich library of theological tomes, written by deeply esteemed godly Christians. These resources provide an essential solid Scriptural foundation for our understanding. By contrast, those reporting these dreams tend to be people whom the world would look down upon. Ken Peters reported that sharing his dream in churches only got him into trouble and so he concentrated instead on being a missionary in Guatemala. Brandon Biggs was a church janitor when he had his Tribulation dream. During His first coming Jesus prayed, "I thank You, Father, Lord of heaven and earth, that You have hidden these things from *the* wise and prudent and have revealed them to babes."[166] Is it possible that this pattern of divine concealment and revelation is being repeated in these latter days leading to the Second Coming? Perhaps, in weighing all this up, we need to be reminded that: "God has chosen the foolish things of the world to put to shame the wise, and God has chosen the weak things of the world to put to shame the things which are mighty."[167] We may want to ask ourselves instead; is it wise to disregard the messages in biblically-tested modern-day dreams and visions? How else could God be expected to increase knowledge in these Last Days? How does the Lord Himself feel about what is ahead? We get an idea of the importance of this matter to Him by the sheer bulk of prophetic verses in the Word of God. It has been estimated that about one-eighth of the Bible still has a future fulfilment.[168]

---

[166] Matthew 11:25
[167] 1 Corinthians 1:27
[168] Got Questions website: "How Much of the Bible is Prophecy?"

Surely, He wants His people to understand and prepare accordingly, to heed voices in the wilderness, however faint, crying out "prepare the way of the Lord."[169]

Mainstream Christian doctrine is clear that salvation is by faith alone.[170] Nevertheless, in considering the implications of the parable of the wise and foolish virgins, I would urge attention to working out our own salvation with fear and trembling.[171] Ponder too on the reason why the Apostle Paul expressed concern about being disqualified after preaching to others,[172] and for James telling us that faith without works is dead.[173] It is not sufficient to proclaim this message of the significance of sanctification and drawing near to the Lord, nor just to believe it. "Even the demons believe—and tremble!"[174] We have to additionally manifest our faith by practical steps to deepen our walk with Him.

For some, the idea of a partial Rapture may raise as many questions as it seeks to address. What degree of unwatchfulness, stubborn sinful ways, compromise and backsliding may disqualify an individual believer from being granted access to the marriage supper? Does the Lord exercise a different level of judgement and grace over His followers in the End Times than upon those who died in Christ previously? Why is there such a paucity of explicit teaching in the Scriptures on the subject? Some things we can only leave with the One who said:

---

[169] Luke 3:4
[170] Got Questions: "Is salvation by faith alone, or by faith plus works?"
[171] Philippians 2:12
[172] 1 Corinthians 9:27
[173] James 2:20
[174] James 2:19b

"for My thoughts are not your thoughts, nor are your ways My ways."[175] As Abraham said to the Lord when he was interceding for Sodom: "shall not the Judge of all the earth do right?"[176] This is also a good opportunity to remind ourselves of the verse we considered in the introduction: "It is the glory of God to conceal a matter, but the glory of kings is to search out a matter."[177]

What should we do?

This interpretation of the Rapture should encourage Christians who look forward to meeting the Lord to pursue peace with all people, and holiness, without which none of us will see the Lord.[178] Is it possible that if Christians are not being purified and set apart now through cleansing and intimacy, then in God's grace, deep love, mercy and patience, He will provide a second chance to be different when facing the Antichrist? Jesus instructs us that not everyone who calls Him Lord will be saved, but only those who do the will of His Father.[179] What is the will of the Father? "For this is the will of God, your sanctification."[180] We are told that the Lord is not willing for any to perish but that all should come to repentance.[181] We

---

[175] Isaiah 55:8-9
[176] Genesis 18:25
[177] Proverbs 25:2
[178] Hebrews 12:14
[179] Matthew 7:21
[180] 1 Thessalonians 4:3a
[181] 2 Peter 3:9

know that no chastening seems to be pleasant or enjoyable at the time, but painful; however, later it yields the peaceable fruit of righteousness to those who have been trained by it.[182] We need to look at this impending suffering and cleansing by fire in light of verses such as: "he who has suffered in the flesh has ceased from sin."[183] "For when Your judgments are in the earth, the inhabitants of the world will learn righteousness."[184]

I have heard lack of holiness likened to a bride who determines to keep a few boyfriends after her marriage to her favourite one.[185] In other words, spiritual adultery. "Adulterers and adulteresses! Do you not know that friendship with the world is enmity with God?"[186] Sanctification following salvation is a process. Some of the Lord's people may need support and personal ministry now to let go of areas of oppression. A good starting point for some is to determine to forgive others, and even themselves, and so be set free from bad fruits such as jealousy, bitterness, anger and self-deprecation. We may turn our thoughts once more to the Shulammite in Song of Solomon chapter 5. She was devastated when she finally opened the door of her chamber, as it was too late to be united with her bridegroom.[187] We should not be discouraged and think that every hesitancy or struggle to obey the Lord instantly condemns us to be reckoned among the foolish virgins. The Lord is looking for us to willingly agree to embark upon,

---

[182] Hebrews 12:11
[183] 1 Peter 4:1
[184] Isaiah 26:9
[185] You Tube video: "Why you are not Experiencing the Presence of God" John Bevere
[186] James 4:4
[187] Song of Solomon 5:6

and then travel along, the journey of obedience and forgiveness. When others have hurt us, we are required to resist the temptation of being entrapped in indignant self-justification. This attitude, once entrenched, leads to a drying up of the oil of intimacy, a hardening of heart, and a distancing in our relationship with God. How easy it is for us, as we lose the sense of His nearness, to seek comfort by immersing ourselves in religious duties like the foolish virgins. We must guard our own hearts, be honest with the Lord about how we are feeling, and exhort one another daily, "lest any of you be hardened through the deceitfulness of sin."[188] Forgiveness is a matter of the will rather than merely reacting to our feelings: "But if you do not forgive men their trespasses, neither will your Father forgive your trespasses."[189]

We may want to work through the love of money, which is the root of all kinds of evil. This causes some to stray from the Faith due to greed, and in turn leads to many griefs.[190] Then, Scripture instructs us that envy and self-interest are manifested in disorder and evil actions.[191] Again, dealing with examples such as these may take time and effort that extends beyond confessing our sins, which of course is the first step in the process. The ministries of the late Derek Prince, and also that of Mike Connell, are both very helpful in this whole area of deliverance.[192] To illustrate this point, consider my garden, where we have an infestation of the weed known as "mare's tails." It

---

[188] Hebrews 3:13
[189] Matthew 6:15
[190] 1 Timothy 6:10
[191] James 3:16
[192] Both have websites and a presence on YouTube. For example: Mike Connell "Overcoming the Root of Bitterness" YouTube

is difficult to eradicate because the roots are so very deep. We too may notice sin patterns in our lives, just as we notice the ugly weeds encroaching on what we choose to grow. But just as the green growth of the mare's tails is only the tip of the iceberg, as it were, so too sin has roots which need addressing so that we can be free. We are set apart for our heavenly Bridegroom, sealed with the promise of the Holy Spirit – whom we must take pains not to grieve.[193] Indeed, we are told in Matthew 7:20 that we each will be known by our fruits.

Many will be familiar with ancient Jewish wedding customs associated with the parable of the wise and foolish virgins. The bridegroom would go away to his father's home to prepare a home for his bride. This betrothal period was for one year.[194] When all was ready, the father would say to his son, "it is time for you to go and collect your bride." The son would not know in advance when the father would announce this, just as the Son of God does not know exactly when He will be returning.[195] The bride waited with readiness with her attendants, not knowing the day nor the hour when he would come back. When the time comes for our heavenly Bridegroom to return to collect us, may we all have in mind the advice in Luke 17:32 to remember Lot's wife. Let us purpose not to look back on unwise virgins and the unsaved, however concerned we may be for them.

[193] Ephesians 1:13, 4:30
[194] Dr. Renald Showers "Jewish Marriage Customs" www.biblestudy-manuals.net/jewish_marriage_customs.htm
[195] Matthew 24:36

"A man who isolates himself seeks his own desire; he rages against all wise judgment."[196] As we see the Day drawing near, we must not neglect meeting together, but consider how to stir one another to love and good works.[197] Wise virgins keep in fellowship with other believers, seeking to preserve the unity of the Spirit in the bond of peace.[198] We need to sever our emotional ties with this world's riches, whether property, vehicles, businesses, or anything else, so that being parted from them will be painless. This is a particular snare to the lukewarm, materialistic end-times Laodicean Church. There is a warning to heed of wailing and misery for those who have hoarded treasure in the Last Days and lived luxuriously on the earth in self-indulgence.[199] Remember the attitude of Moses in Egypt who preferred to suffer alongside the people of God, rather than enjoy the fleeting pleasures of sin, because he looked for the reward.[200] As pointed out by John Bevere in his book, "Drawing Near – A Life of Intimacy with God," Moses would rather have endured the privations of the wilderness than miss the very *presence* of God.[201] May the things of this world grow strangely dim in the light of His glory and grace![202] How much better to focus on the return of the One who has gone to His Father's house. There are many rooms there and He has gone to prepare a special place for each of us![203]

---

[196] Proverbs 18:1
[197] Hebrews 10:25
[198] Ephesians 4:3
[199] James 5:1-5
[200] Hebrews 11:25-26
[201] Exodus 33:15-16
[202] Hymn "Turn Your Eyes upon Jesus" Helen Lemmel 1918
[203] John 14:2-3

As a wise young friend observed, it is far more important to be ready for the Rapture than to understand all the details. Let us reflect upon the warning: "If anyone does not abide in Me, he is cast out as a branch and is withered; and they gather them and throw *them* into the fire, and they are burned."[204] Study afresh the account of Mary and Martha, in which Mary spent time at the feet of Jesus listening to and admiring Him, whereas Martha was preoccupied with service and resented her more contemplative sister. "Martha, Martha, you are worried and troubled about many things. But one thing is needed, and Mary has chosen that good part, which will not be taken away from her."[205] Does this account have an additional end-times perspective? Could Mary represent the wise virgins investing time in being close to the Lord? Another candidate for this group is the Apostle John, who is referred to as the disciple whom Jesus loved.[206] We may puzzle as to how John developed this especially close relationship with Jesus. We may speculate that John was drawn to spend more time alone with the Lord than, say, impetuous Peter. We know that, ultimately, John was given the privilege of taking care of the Saviour's mother, as well as being entrusted with the visions and anointing to write the Book of Revelation as a very aged man. Our relationship with the Lord must come first in our lives as Christians – an essential requirement for effective and fruitful service for the Lord. "For no other foundation can anyone lay than that which is laid, which is Jesus Christ."[207] As the hymn says: "How firm a foundation, ye saints of the Lord, is laid for

---

[204] John 15:6
[205] Luke 10:42
[206] John 13:23, 19:26
[207] See 1 Corinthians 3:11-15

your faith in God's excellent Word!"[208] We are in the Last Days of deception, with false prophets arising to show great signs and wonders in order to mislead even the elect, if it were possible.[209] Stay close to the Lord and be discerning, and anticipate that internet platforms such as YouTube will undoubtedly include false prophets. How essential it is to be noble-minded like the Bereans, eagerly examining the Scriptures[210] to see if the teachings and messages we encounter about the End Times are so. The apostle Peter clearly tells us "that no prophecy of Scripture is of any private interpretation."[211] How vital it is for us to be led by the Holy Spirit in unravelling the prophetic Scriptures!

The book of Proverbs has much to say about wisdom and foolishness: "Get wisdom! Get understanding! ... she will preserve you; love her, and she will keep you. Wisdom is the principal thing; therefore get wisdom."[212] The rest of the book of Proverbs has much to teach about wisdom. The fear of the Lord is the first step in this journey.[213] What better motivation for the virgins in these End Times than to ensure that they are eligible for the wedding feast? We are encouraged to fellowship with the wise and to keep our distance from the foolish.[214] We should be wary of simply figuring things out in our own minds rather than factoring in the advice of others.[215] We

---

[208] R. Keen 1787
[209] Matthew 24:24
[210] Acts 17:11
[211] 2 Peter 1:20
[212] Proverbs 4:5-7
[213] Proverbs 1:7
[214] Proverbs 13:20
[215] Proverbs 12:15, 18:2, 28:26

should be teachable.[216] The wise avoid needless quarrels with the foolish.[217] We need to be humble and listen to others: "A fool has no delight in understanding, but in expressing his own heart."[218] We need to be slow to speak and slow to anger.[219] It can be summarised in the verses: "Trust in the Lord with all your heart, and lean not on your own understanding; in all your ways acknowledge Him, and He shall direct your paths."[220] Later in the same chapter we read, "the wise shall inherit glory, but shame shall be the legacy of fools."[221] Does this verse have eschatological significance? What deep shame to be excluded from the marriage supper of the Lamb. The sound of the trumpet blast (*shofar* in Hebrew) will issue forth immediately prior to the departure of the wise virgins at the Rapture.[222] Those left behind, who know their Bibles well, will understand all too clearly the awful situation into which they will then suddenly be plunged. They will know that he who restrains is then removed, paving the way for the Antichrist.[223] I have heard various interpretations over the years as to the identity of the restrainer. These vary from the Holy Spirit, to the raptured body of Christ, to the archangel Michael. It does not take much imagination to envisage the anarchic and alarming state of an unrestrained society.

---

216 Proverbs 9:9, 15:2
217 Proverbs 20:3, 29:9
218 Proverbs 18:2
219 Proverbs 14:29, 29:11,20
220 Proverbs 3:5-6
221 Proverbs 3:35
222 1 Thessalonian 4:16
223 2 Thessalonians 2:7

Some of the foolish virgins surely will know that they deserved to miss out. There may be heartfelt cries from the bitter disappointment of being excluded from the Lord's reaping of the righteous: "Harvest is past, summer is ended, and we are not saved."[224] The exhortation of Jesus is most relevant: "Behold, I am coming as a thief. Blessed is he who watches, and keeps his garments, lest he walk naked and they see his shame."[225] If we are not wakeful, watchful, prayerful and suitably attired in readiness for One who will come when we are not expecting Him, like a thief, then we will be deeply ashamed. Instead let us be wisely prepared in readiness in order to enjoy the marriage supper of the Lamb: "Blessed are those servants whom the master, when he comes, will find watching. Assuredly, I say to you that he will gird himself and have them sit down to eat, and will come and serve them."[226]

We can look in the Scriptures for other mentions of the wise and foolish. We read in Matthew 7 of the wise man building his house upon the rock and that house surviving the ravages of savage weather. By contrast, the foolish man's house collapses under the same conditions because it was built on the sand. Does this parable have special end-times significance? May each of us be able to discern between the rock and the sand! We must evaluate our personal stock of oil. In ancient Bible times, olive oil had many uses other than lighting and heating. It was also used for healing wounds and, generally, for

[224] Jeremiah 8:20
[225] Revelation 16:15
[226] Luke 12:37

protecting and nourishing the skin and scalp.[227] We see the former use in the parable of the Good Samaritan in Luke 10. If we have wounds which still hurt because of bad experiences in the past, or if we feel spiritually dry, then this is a nudge to immerse ourselves more in the oil of the Holy Spirit and to bring His light to our problem areas in life.

We need deep courage and commitment to the Lord to face these days ahead, and this applies to both the wise and also to the foolish virgins who go on to overcome during the Tribulation. These are days, as mentioned, when many will be offended.[228] We must avoid the trap of feeling offence towards the Lord about the special challenges presented to us as last-days believers. We are obliged to trust God's plans for the winding up of the age: "blessed is he who is not offended because of Me."[229] We need to ponder on Mordecai's advice to Esther: "who knows whether you have come to the kingdom for such a time as this."[230] We are surrounded by the great cloud of witnesses,[231] and this includes Christians from Ancient Rome who suffered gruesome deaths under Nero, and those like the Ten Boom family who willingly sacrificed their lives to protect Jewish people in World War II, as well as a multitude of modern-day martyrs. "Let us therefore come

---

[227] Bibletools.org – Forerunner Commentary "What the Bible says about Olive Oil"
[228] Matthew 24:10 KJ, NKJV, Amplified, Darby, Webster etc
[229] Matthew 11:6
[230] Esther 4:14
[231] Hebrews 12:1

boldly to the throne of grace, that we may obtain mercy and find grace to help in time of need."[232]

Concluding thoughts

Consider the other parables in the Olivet Discourse[233] that provide the context for the teaching of the 10 virgins. There is the lesson of the fig tree, the wise and the wicked servant, the talents, and the sheep and goats. They are all part of Jesus' response to His disciples when asked for further details about the Last Days.[234] The fig tree, whose branches become tender and put out leaves, is Israel, back in her land and budding since 1948. The relatively recent fulfilment of this sign indicates that we are already in the season of His return. The wicked servant does not take his master's instructions seriously because he does not truly believe that he to whom he is accountable is returning soon. This attitude of heart leads to his disgraceful behaviour and abusive treatment of his fellow servants. The lazy servant in the parable of the talents has no desire to please his master. Despite being entrusted with his master's wealth, he fearfully refuses to invest it. The final parable about the sheep and goats is rather different. It concerns caring for the needy in these precarious Last Days and may ultimately refer to how, during the Tribulation, believers treat Jewish people, the brothers of Jesus.

---

[232] Hebrews 4:16
[233] Matthew 24-25
[234] Matthew 24:3

You may like to meditate on the Song of Solomon, thanking the Lord for the passion He has for us, His bride.[235] Accept the depth of love He has for each one of us, however dark we may feel. Take time to express your love for Him, and how you too long to go away with Him. This book of the Bible has a special message for the end-times *ecclesia*.[236] Some Christians will have a hard time even accepting that others love them, let alone Almighty God. This may be due to a dysfunctional childhood and upbringing, or a result of the hurt of being treated badly in relationships as an adult. Others will not be familiar with relationships based on love and spending time together, rather than on carrying out expected duties and tasks. Such a background inevitably erodes a believer's sense of self-worth. This in turn causes people to believe the lie that they are neither good enough nor deserving of being loved, especially by Almighty God. Yet others will feel most secure in being loved from their earliest days and throughout adulthood, and do not feel the need to bask in the love of their Heavenly Father and their Saviour. Their emotional tanks are already comfortably full! Whichever camp we are in, there is the same need to ask the Lord to awaken love in our relationship with Him, meditating not on our feelings or inclinations, but on verses like, "In this is love, not that we loved God, but that He loved us and sent His Son to be the propitiation for our sins."[237] "But God demonstrates His own love toward us, in that while we

---

[235] Song of Solomon 4:1-15
[236] a called-out assembly or congregation, commonly translated "church" "What is the definition of ekklesia?" Got Questions.org
[237] 1 John 4:10

were still sinners, Christ died for us."[238] Partaking of communion, or the Lord's Supper, is a wonderful opportunity to reflect on the depths of love which God has for each one of us, His people.

Some of us need to grow from a mindset of merely singing hymns and Christian choruses, to using them to express our worship and devotion to our heavenly Bridegroom. Others may develop their Bible reading into an opportunity to hear what the Lord has to say to them personally. May we all be among those who grow in demonstrating our love for the Lord, and not being critical or judgemental of believers who express this, remembering God's punishment of Michal, the wife of David, who sneered at his exuberant dancing before the Lord.[239] Developing our relationship with the Lord is a two-way process, involving both speaking to Him in prayer and worship and listening to Him. The parable of the wise and foolish virgins is a challenge to each one of us to stop focussing on our Christian activities and ministry for the Lord at the expense of our relationship with Him.

Once we are born again into the family of God, the Holy Spirit commences His ongoing role to sanctify us completely so that we may be ready for the second coming of the Messiah.[240] At times this can be a painful process as, like with Israel, God may allow suffering to accomplish His purpose: "Behold, I have refined you, but not as silver; I have tested you in the furnace of affliction."[241] He already knows all about us, and

[238] Romans 5:8
[239] 2 Samuel 6:14-22
[240] 1 Thessalonians 5:23
[241] Isaiah 48:10

tests us so that we may become aware of the inward sin lurking in our hearts and then repent. This is the dross that rises to the surface while we are in that furnace. Listen to how the Lord described this process in the book of Isaiah: "I will turn My hand against you, and thoroughly purge away your dross, and take away all your alloy."[242] He elaborates about the impurities removed during the process of purifying silver to Ezekiel – copper, tin, iron and lead.[243] Let us guard our hearts and, like good soldiers enlisted by the Lord, not get entangled with the concerns of this world, so that we can please the One who called us.[244] May we not complain inwardly that we have been dealt bad cards in life, but instead see such arduous circumstances as our own personal challenge to overcome in order to gain a future reward commensurate with our heart's attitude to difficulties: "that in the *ages to come* He might show the exceeding riches of His grace in *His* kindness toward us in Christ Jesus."[245] What motivation this is to "let all bitterness, wrath, anger, clamor, and evil speaking be put away from you, with all malice. And be kind to one another, tenderhearted, forgiving one another, even as God in Christ forgave you."[246]

What a privilege wise virgins are offered to be caught up while still alive, to marvel at their instantaneous bodily change, and to not face death! "We shall not all sleep, but we shall all be changed— in a moment, in the twinkling of an eye, at the last trumpet. For the trumpet will sound, and the dead will be

---

[242] Isaiah 1:25
[243] Ezekiel 22:18
[244] 2 Timothy 2:4
[245] Ephesians 2:7, author's emphasis.
[246] Ephesians 4:31-32

raised incorruptible, and we shall be changed. For this corruptible must put on incorruption, and this mortal must put on immortality."[247] May we, as end-times virgins, take to heart the admonition that we reap what we sow.[248] Let us be lavish in devoting time to worship, prayer, fasting, deliverance from sin and oppression, sanctification and fellowship to make ourselves ready. May we all know what it is to "take time to be holy."[249] Let each one of us say, like John the Baptist, "He must increase, but I must decrease."[250] May we hear the heartfelt anguished plea from the Lord to separate ourselves from the Babylonish world system before it is too late, "Come out of her, my people, lest you share in her sins, and lest you receive of her plagues."[251]

Finally, may we co-labour with God to do our part in preparing the corporate bride of our Messiah. May we all be granted opportunities to share the need to prepare for the Rapture with those He lays on our hearts, so that we may be among those "who are wise [who] shall shine like the brightness of the firmament, and those who turn many to righteousness like the stars forever and ever."[252] Be inspired by the exhortation of the Apostle Paul to forget that which is behind and press on toward the goal for the prize of the *upward call* of God in our Lord Jesus.[253] May we increasingly perceive our

---

[247] 1 Corinthians 15:51-53
[248] Galatians 6:7
[249] Words from famous hymn "Take Time to be Holy" by William D. Longstaff 1822-1894
[250] John 3:30
[251] Revelation 18:4
[252] Daniel 12:3
[253] Philippians 3:14 (author's emphasis)

sinful attitudes and actions as ugly stains to be removed from the beautiful wedding gown we aspire to wear one day. And may we be obedient to the Scriptures, praying that we will be counted worthy to escape what is ahead, and willingly embrace the particular process of sanctification which the Lord deems appropriate to our individual circumstances and calling.

Let each of us seek to draw near to God, and He will draw near to us.[254] Our chief joy and focus should be close fellowship with the Lord. "Whom have I in heaven *but You*? And *there is* none upon earth *that* I desire besides You."[255] The Apostle Paul wrote of his deepest desire: "That *I may know him*, and the power of his resurrection, and the fellowship of his sufferings, being made conformable unto his death."[256] Even if we are among the most devout students of Scripture, the written *logos,* we need to treasure and build our relationship with the Word who became flesh.[257] We may yearn for heaven, a place where we will sin no more, be with our saved loved ones, and experience what eye has not seen nor ear heard.[258] However, primarily we should be longing for everlasting fellowship with the Lord. He promises to be *with us* until the end of the age.[259] "Then we who are alive *and* remain shall be caught up together with them in the clouds to meet the Lord in the air. And *thus we shall always be with the Lord.*"[260] Approaching the soon-coming Rapture and avoiding the appalling

---

[254] James 4:8

[255] Psalm 73:25

[256] Philippians 3:10, author's emphasis

[257] John 1:14

[258] 1 Corinthians 2:9

[259] Matthew 28:20

[260] 1 Thessalonians 4:17, author's emphasis

seven-year tribulation ahead is deep motivation for us to be diligent to make sure of our calling and election so that we will never stumble.[261] It is time to lift up our heads because our redemption is drawing near![262] The ancient Jewish wedding celebrations lasted seven days, or one *week*. A pre-tribulation Rapture allows for the marriage supper in heaven during the final *week* of Daniel. Let us aspire to be there!

Prayer of Salvation

Heavenly Father, thank you for sending the Lord Jesus Christ, Your divine precious Son, God in the flesh, to die on the Cross to pay the penalty for my sins. I deserve an eternal and dreadful punishment for my wrongdoings, yet You have saved me through Your sacrifice. Please forgive me for all my sins, for the ways I have offended You in my actions, words and thoughts. I believe that Your Son is alive because He rose from the dead on the third day, and I open the door of my heart to You Lord Jesus and ask You to come into my life through the Holy Spirit and be my Saviour and Lord. Help me to know the next stage in this journey of faith and repentance and lead me in living for You.

In Jesus' name, Amen.

---

[261] 2 Peter 1:10
[262] Luke 21:28

Hymn: Take Time to be Holy

Take time to be holy, speak oft with thy Lord;
Abide in Him always, and feed on His Word.
Make friends of God's children, help those who are weak,
Forgetting in nothing His blessing to seek.

Take time to be holy, the world rushes on;
Spend much time in secret, with Jesus alone.
By looking to Jesus, like Him thou shalt be;
Thy friends in thy conduct His likeness shall see.

Take time to be holy, let Him be thy Guide;
And run not before Him, whatever betide.
In joy or in sorrow, still follow the Lord,
And, looking to Jesus, still trust in His Word.

Take time to be holy, be calm in thy soul,
Each thought and each motive beneath His control.
Thus led by His Spirit to fountains of love,
Thou soon shalt be fitted for service above.

William D. Longstaff 1822-1894

Exploring the End Times and Interceding for Israel

Rosamund Weissman

Dark clouds are drawing ever nearer to Israel, as the storm brews up around her, and the Time of Jacob's Trouble approaches.

Those who pray for Israel do not need a book with formulated prayers. That is the role of the Holy Spirit. What is needed is written material to illuminate the mystery ahead, both for Israel and for the whole world. The Lord will do the rest.

Setting the scene for the Time of Jacob's Trouble is best approached with an eye for detail. This background will show us how to engage with the subject of the End Times and will help us to focus on the people of Jacob. It is a struggle to pray into a situation which we find mysterious.

Jesus tells us to watch and pray; for this we require understanding about what we are watching out for. We need to discern the significance of what is happening on the world stage, as well as what is on the horizon for Israel.

Through explanations about the End Times and glimpses into Israeli society, you will find it easier to connect with Israel in prayer in these last days.

Available via fresholivepress.com

Hebrew Lessons for Beginners from the New Testament

Rosamund Weissman

This is written for Christians who want to learn Hebrew and who desire to deepen their understanding of the Hebraic background of the New Testament. This teaching is humbly offered to contribute towards "the equipping of the saints for the work of ministry, for the edifying of the body of Christ."

The New Testament contains a treasury of Hebrew thoughts and truths, thinly concealed beneath the so-familiar text. These gems are presented and examined through the medium of 12 beginners' Hebrew lessons. Each lesson can be approached in one of two ways. They are suitable for those who wish to learn or revise beginner's Hebrew. Alternatively, the English text can be read and appreciated in its own right (making use of the transliterations), without studying the Hebrew reading component. Whether you are reading this book to build up your knowledge of biblical or modern Hebrew, or to inspire you in poetry, song, or craft activities, may you be blessed!

Available via fresholivepress.com